SPOKEN WORD   MAY 21 2002

Freedom Papers
HPJ's Writeeasy Publishing
ISBN (Trade pbk.)
0615598277

Layout and Design: Chris Massenburg
Cover Art: Vonnie Perry
Inner Art: Anonymous

HPJ's Writeeasy Publishing
Durham, North Carolina

www.dasanahanu.com

To Melina,
I hope that
you are inspired!

Dariush
Ahan

Freedom Papers

Table of Contents

Captain's Cry

The day has come
A chance to be more than fear
More than hurt
A chance to hold hope
Grasp our pride
To dream
Be this day
Live this day
Breathe in the time
Exhale the truth
We the true ones
Have no more doubt
The horn sounds for us
The ticking clock has laid its hands on this moment
Change is near
We live or we die
Free

Dyslexic

He seemed to always get things backwards
Like the "I Love You" that found his lips
After she closed the door
He tattooed an open door over his heart
So he wouldn't forget again
But now he goes in and out of relationships
Unable to shut out his fears of commitment

There is a small empty studio apartment in his chest
With no furniture and hardwood floors
Feng Shui feels fraudulent
Because he's not comfortable with whom he is
He spends his afternoons in bars like Ikea
Searching for someone who fits

He seems to get things mixed up
Like the cubicle that should have been a dream
Hideaway that should have been a home
Acquaintances like Section 8 housing
Always on his bad side
Felt they couldn't afford to be his friend
Private, closed off, rigid
Providing no assistance
Couldn't allow them close to where his heart lived
They may bring down the value

It started when he was a child
His world beautifully placed
Full of surprises, disparate

Until they told him it was confusion
He replied that the stories were riddles
He was supposed to solve them like Oedipus
They said he had a complex
He said he didn't have no motherfucking problem
They disliked the difference between his understandings
And his achievement
Labeled him developmentally disabled
Called his parents and told them their child was dyslexic
He didn't open a book again for 4 years

He got good at mimicking
Life imitating art
But this wasn't realism
It was an abstract impression of fitting in
He Jackson Pollock'd High School
Framed it as a necessary evil
Exhibiting no remorse
Until needles pricked his skin
Painting heroin hued portraits in pointillism
A fanatic Seurat working with a withering canvas
He was addicted for 4 years

4 years out of rehab he found the answer
Figured out how to read the pages in the novel existence
God had written for him

He's dyslexic
Has always had trouble reading
Reverses letters and numbers
Struggled with symbols

But he believes he is better this way
Without the preconceived notions of this world
Wrote his lost love a letter
Said he knows now that love is still possible
Because U and I isn't any less gratifying reversed

Traded in his cubicle for a Barnes & Nobles badge
Books are his life now
So he perfect binds days
That begin and end the same way
With a prayer
This faithful autobiography self published
Printed on daydreams
Distributed in his smile

He used to wonder
If God broke apart his world
To test his faith or his ingenuity
But he has found the glue
To piece his peace back together

A modern day Aesop
Who dove off the cliff of self-doubt
With rebellion on his tongue
So that the fable of his fight
Could inspire the next dreamer
To believe in happy endings

He seemed to always get things backwards
Like the "Fuck You" that found his lips
12 years after the world tried to tell him

God's craftsmanship was defective
He tattooed a middle finger on his upper arm
So that when he gave doubters the cold shoulder
They would know why

There is a small studio apartment in his chest
Furnished with hope and accented with determination
Feng Shui feels like freedom
He has become comfortable with who he is
So now he spends his afternoons in bookstores
Searching for an adventure that fits

Fly

There are two small eyes full of hope
Sitting on a grey stoop
Perched ready for flight
A young bird waiting to be fed encouragement
And taught how to spread his wings

He sits here hungry
Because sitting at an empty dinner table hurts more
Outside is larger than his cupboard
And he believes he can find something of substance out here
So he spreads his smile between passing greetings
And bites into should be

This is his daily meal
This young bird nested in front of despair
He doesn't want to live in there
So he brings his hope out here
How long till he flies
How long until the skies become his haven
Wind beneath his wings
I want his wishes to come true

We have a ritual
Everyday that I find him on that stoop
I stop and we talk
I bring two sandwiches and a bag of chips
Then before our goodbyes are exchanged
I tell him to stand and spread his arms to the side
"What are you doing now?"
"Flying," he says
I make him promise to never forget that

I took it for granted

Like fanciful feathers caged in society's living room
Wool pulled over our recognition putting our morals to sleep
I expected that he would be there
Everyday I passed that stoop
Repeating revelations like he was God's parakeet
Until I realized that hunters find thrills on inner city blocks
Looking for pheasants that should be considered royalty
Yes it was foul
That the news considered him the stray
Not the bullet that took him away
But it was his dreams
That called him to that grey stoop each day
Perched ready for flight
Shot down
Now kisses head skyward
As tears stain concrete
And I feel responsible
Feel like I doomed him to downfall
Two sandwiches and chips ain't worth lost hope
Two sandwiches and chips ain't worth someone's soul
I would have rather put a spread on his table
And have him spread his smile to me now
But I wanted him to believe he could fly
Now I have to hold his mother and hear her ask why

The Pastor spoke eloquently
Said that boy was an angel
Who knew it was only a matter of time
Before he was headed home
Built that nest by gathering fondness and admiration
That became a wreath of faith
Hung on the wretchedness of that tenement
When he was gone
That boy wanted to fly

And Heaven was waiting for his arrival

I listened to that choir sing
Knew that God had finally given him his wings
And I felt ashamed
That all I had to offer an angel
Were two sandwiches and a bag of chips
Now two doves and a lamb may have been given to atone
But two sandwiches and a bag of chips can't forgive my sins
I can cry for a reason but it won't bring him back again

I miss him
Because he made me believe in beautiful
Believe in maybe
And that's so important for a man
Walking through a concrete jungle
Full of cynicism and doubt

Now I have a ritual
I walk past that stoop
Stop and step up onto that grey launching pad
Eat two sandwiches and a bag of chips
Then I stand and spread my arms out to the side
I vision what hope looks like as I close my eyes
Then I open them and turn my head to the sky
Tell me young man I say
What are you doing now?
I feel a calm come over me as I begin to cry
Then I smile with tears falling from my eyes
When I hear the wind whisper his reply
I knew you would never forget that
Fly...Fly...Fly

Introspection

I can't breathe
Sweating
Shoulders weakening
Each moment heavy
I don't know if I can save you
Don't know if I can write
Redemption
I worry if Peter will be the last
To hear my feeble attempt
To speak salvation
Before returning me to the hell
I feel now
Pitching my tent
In purgatory

What are my words worth
Is it the placement or the position
Between a hypnotic melody
Behind the pulpit of an altar
In the midst of white pages
Like eloquent elitism
Or amidst the smoke
Of a coffee house
Like pre packaged commodity
Are they more acceptable
If they fit within a certain context
If so
I'll country club my conviction
And gate my community consciousness

I worry
That I'll wake up tomorrow
To realize I was only significant
In my dreams
I'm afraid of insomnia
Praying for narcolepsy
So I can unexpectedly become
Something

I want to pen towards promise
Not perdition
Putting passion into each stroke
Because this indulgence
Is better than indiscretion
Mistakenly
Putting passion into each stroke
Either way I lust to matter

I'm scared
That I have done nothing
Given everything
Can't write anything
But storm clouds

I fear
There isn't anything
In these notebooks
But hallucinations
That instead of using
My creative imagination

I have imagined my creativity

I'm terrified
That there is no reflection in the mirror
That I was bitten by a desire to matter
Sucking the sincerity and honesty from my words
Leaving me searching the darkness
For affirmation
Running from the light that can illuminate my insecurities

I am concerned
That I have costumed myself a poet
Believing spotlights are calling me
That the dark night's mystery
Will become hated rather than respected
Tell Tim Burton to script me significant
Direct me to the self-assurance
That this is what I am destined to be

Jesus Wept

The house on 510 Maple Street
Wasn't more than wood and hopes
Last refuge for a couple who lost their faith
Long before they lost their way
And found themselves living where demons come to play
Mary just wanted piece of mind and the rumors to end
Reputation left in pieces
Because the end of John's fist left imprints
And bruises and gossip go hand in hand
Prayed for deliverance but instead found herself in delivery
John liked to leave his seed after he left his mark
Mary pained not from the whole of what was in her womb
But the hole in her heart
And the realization of what her child will have to go through
She named him David
A blessing

Felt that she should've married her a Joseph
Her John was no Baptist
But the angels found her anyway
Daydreamed that the baby was not of his father
It was Immaculate Conception
Prayed that the heavenly spirit would be his protection
Because she had to leave the hospital
That baby renewed her devotion
John tried to break her spirit
He broke ribs, jaws, arms, fingers, but not her faith
11 years later a new target had taken her place
Got smarter and never hit the boy in the face
Daddy just tattooed secrets on his skin

You can't heckle harm

When the devil likes to hear you scream
So voices stayed silent and eyes stayed closed
Even though it left a bad feeling in their gut
But eyes were bruised and lips were swollen shut
John Chapter 1 (fist) verse 5 (fingers)
Says the light shines through darkness

And the darkness can never extinguish it
Did this explain the stars David saw after this one sided fight
This ain't right
Because the text in the book is so different

Than what he goes through every night
Why would God create this madness and engulf him in it
Just praying for his father to be finished
David's hope is broken
Now his soul is lame
Feels he was just calling God's name in vain
Praying for sunshine but only getting rain

See this is the house where Jesus wept
Because it was Mary not Lazarus who fell down
Left that boy alone
Four days later had that boy in black at his mother's funeral
Jesus was calling her home
Soon after that they took David to a foster home
They took John in handcuffs, but it was David who was shackled
To the dysfunction of a house full of lost sheep
A janitor name Saul who tried to take him in his sleep

The only thing this home fostered was blasphemy
David being touched in the darkness of the night
Feeling taunted by the sun, as if it highlighted his nightmare
He knew pain so when he heard the punishment if he told
He kept the fondling and fellatio a secret to his soul

That day by day was growing more and more cold
Felt that someone has to notice
This brown penny with a finger in his hole he felt hopeless

See this was the house where Jesus Wept
It was 10:14 when Mark knocked on his door
Bible in his hand
Said that Jesus saw what was happening
And was very displeased
Took David's hand and pulled him down to his knees
Said the Kingdom of God belongs to such as these
I assure you, anyone who doesn't have their kind of faith
Will never get into the Kingdom of God

Mark promised David he'd stay by his side
So they prepared for a battle
Rain falling outside
But Saul never arrived
They woke the next morning with joy in their eyes
Felt washed in a new beginning
I guess it was the anointing of Jesus' cries

Saul had been discovered
The police came and took him away
David's grandmother had been discovered
She was on her way
When she arrived
It was as if David had been crowned king of a new day
For that lost herd of sheep pinned in, he was an inspiration
But it was his grandmother who spoke
And offered this revelation
For the Lamb who stands in front of the throne
Will be their Shepherd
He will lead them to the springs of life-giving water

And God will wipe away all their tears

David walked out the front door with his head up high
Waved goodbye to his guardian angel still standing inside
Grabbed his grandmother's hand
Felt hope renewed inside
Turned his head to the sky
And Jesus wept
Grey clouds dripping wet affirmation on their skins
The rain was never more welcome
As if Jesus was saying you're welcome
David turned to that house
Picked up a rock and slung it with pride
Feeling like he was killing that Goliath
Holding all his nightmares held inside
Wrapped his arms around himself
Like his mother would've done
Tears falling from his eyes
And in recognition of his deliverance
Both Jesus and David cried

Judgment

I.

He stands in this courtroom
Nervous, hands shaking
Wonders if this will be the moment
When he is found guilty
Dressed clean
His spirit still filthy
Suited for this moment of judgment
His defense attorney making her case
Hands clasped together
Spent nights in the book
Looking for precedence
Now she's delivering a statement
Calling for a witness
He sits silent
Facing the bench
Looking this robed figure in the eyes
Hoping he can altar the outcome
Prosecution is the pain in his soul
Lifestyle taking its toll
Temper that had got out of control
He wanted forgiveness
She was willing to settle for grace
He was the subject, predicate felon
Felt like too many people were on his case
Pressure
Linked to his character like a preposition
His deposition

Was that he was tied to the streets
Wanted redemption for his testimony
Salvation for his release
Conjunction's function was apathy
And, so
Now this subject is agreeing
To verbalize his remorse
Seeking a new course
Facing a life sentence
Throwing himself at the mercy of a higher force
Deliberators searching
Seeking the right hymn
Seeing the light in him
Grandmother speaking faithfully
Pastor speaking passionately
Choir singing graciously
He waited anxiously
Pastor's hand to his forehead like a gavel
They grabbed his arms
To take him into custody
He tensed reluctantly
Hearing that redemption
Would require conviction
But gave in knowing it was his insecurities
That made him resist
They held onto him
The Holy Spirit anointed him
The pastor prayed
He was saved
Felt deliverance in his midst

II.

She stands in this courtroom
Accused
Of a crime she didn't commit
Knows it is mistaken identity
She's fighting relentlessly to get the charges dismissed
This is her hearing
Although no one
Is listening to her side of the story
Prosecution has been laid to rest
Hands X'd across his chest
She sees it as a signature
Of his illiterate understanding
He could never read her right
She can still remember the look on his face
Like judgment was his birthright
Her public defender is clueless
Too sensitive to the other side
They say a mother's love is unconditional
But she saw fine print in her mother's eyes
Tells her she should accept a plea
This woman isn't proclaiming innocence
But she damn sure isn't responsible
The jury could take that how they please
They called her a disgrace
Said she murdered a good man
When she broke his heart
She said his expectations were unrealistic
It was either be true to her dreams
Or allow his demanding ways to tear her apart

Dream catcher
Who tried to take her true wealth
Dream merchant
Who bartered her hopes for nightmares
His little princess saw through his fables
Learned to write a happy ending for herself
The judge just sits
Face full of tension
From years of watching her family
Operate like this
Everyone dressed up for the occasion
Wearing the black
Her father will be forever trapped in
She wore pastels
Said she would never be trapped
By darkness again
Albatross medallion around her neck
Her Mother was a product of this oppressive state
What kind of defense could she expect
Her grandmother silences the room
Says how dare you try to convict her
On insufficient evidence
When no one ever bothered
To do a thorough investigation
Of that child's heart and soul
She was never read her rights
Just held under the wrongful will of you people
You can't blame her
For fighting for her own sense of control
Right then she was acquitted
But there was no rejoicing

No cheers or handclaps
Tells them to not worry
She won't ever be coming back
Out the front door
This exonerated butterfly goes
Shuts the door and gasps
Determined to put this all in the past
Turns to the doors of that courthouse
Leaves her necklace on the front doorstep
Laughs

Lost Ones

In a small town in Northern Uganda
A young man is taken through a ritual
In order to spiritually manipulate his loyalty

While in a city in North America
A young man listens to his grandmother sing spirituals
Hoping to spiritually manipulate his blessings

His mother has been cast aside
His sister has become a slave to men's desires

No…his mother has been caught in castes
Labeled as low income
His sister has become the object of men's desires

He has been given a gun and a cause
Now a rebel in the Lord's Resistance Army
Whose only pause is in death

There is a gun waiting for him on the streets
A pawn that has never been taught the cause
But understands the effects

See these are the lost ones
Left in turmoil behind a man made wall of anonymity
Because we refuse to recognize their circumstance
So the next best thing to come
Becomes the worst thing that could happen
We watch it happen

And wait for someone else to take action
But what happens
When they decide to act like they're grown
When a battlefield or a jail cell is where they call home

A mother bird built a nest in the light outside my front door
I guess she felt her children were safest
At home with a poet
But it's funny
There were more little ones waiting to greet me there
Than in some of the after school writing workshops
I've done this year

Where is our little Bob Kaufman, Amiri Baraka, Jane Cortez
Writing to their own beat
With their powerful black pen
Chronicling their artful movement
Surrealism filling their imagination with possibilities
As they stanza their steps in dub
Making their own path
Finding their own way

Can't you see?
We have a responsibility to our children
To make sure that daydreams are possibilities
That their lion, witch, and wardrobe is a great adventure
Not a cowardly president, a resentful lady liberty
And the dressings of misguided commodity
Passed off as culture
I want them to believe in Hogwarts
College campuses where you can learn to use magic

Spells called networking, marketing, and critical thinking
Institutions with chambers of secrets
Like societies, class privilege, and money manipulation
We have to teach them to be explorers
Able to navigate the inner workings of the system
Map them a possibility
Tell them that if they are willing to take the steps
Success is waiting for their arrival

To save our kids we have to get hands on
Calloused from holding on to dreams of their success
Tired from building foundations for them to stand on
Redecorating hearts that are houses for love
Tilling fields where seeds are planted
So that insight can grow organically
Worn hands, our hands, your hands…

Hands we put on the backside of any one out of line
On the shoulder of anyone needing encouragement
On the head of a teary eyed tomorrow
Finding comfort in your arms
On the book that changed your life
That you know they should read
Hand it to them so they know you believe
In seeing them succeed
Because you know how bad this world can be

In a small town in northern Uganda
A young man has a gun and a mission
He has been forced into the pits of hell

While in a city in North America
A young man with drive and ambition
Is given a devil's product to sell

We see him on the streets and we see him on the news
We don't help him or guide him
We call him lost and confused
We don't protect him and we don't love him
We leave him battered and bruised

We won't change their conditions
We won't better their lives
We won't feed them and we won't teach them
So they struggle to survive
With anguish in their heart and hate in their eyes
Trying by any means to conquer the inadequacy felt inside
Full of ambivalence toward a God that made this true
What happens when one day you meet
Their gun is pointed straight at you

Now your hands are raised
Those same hands you could've used to fight for a change
Quiver in fear
You're overcome with shame
Hoping for mercy
But what are you going to do
When they ask
Why should they have mercy on you?

In a small town in Northern Uganda
In a small city in North America

They've lost their innocence
Found no hope
When their final destination
Is handcuffs
Or a pool of blood where their body now floats

So you can do nothing and complain
Watch their struggle from afar
Claim you want to help
But never go where they are
Condemn them and judge them
As you say you'll include them when you pray
Forgetting the possibility
That they may be your jury on judgment day

How can we afford not to find an answer
Are we willing to pay the cost?
When our apathy and ignorance
Is the reason that they're lost
These lost ones

Male Escort

I'm a whore
I sleep with promise for a price
In service of a pimp
Some say cares nothing about me

Stays distant
Like the eyes of a mime who wishes
He could tell me the truth
Like a comatose dream
Everyone hopes will wake up one day

She found me getting off a train of thought
Lost looking for an answer
Taught me how to make money
Standing on my ancestors' shoulders
With my legs in the air

I want her to call my name
So I spend all night
With my head between this weight on my shoulders
Trying to bring my purpose closer to coming true
A forefather's foreplay
With my forefinger searching for an answer

I ain't desperate, I'm submissive
Bound to my calling, disciplined in determination
Dominated by desire to matter
Yesterday has a power over me
Tomorrow can't free me from

But sometimes
I want to tell history I don't want to be
Her whore anymore

All she does is hold my past against me
Tells me
I ain't fit for nothing else
I gotta work off this debt to my ancestry
The world is infatuated
Heard we was hung
They wanna know what black angst feels like
Talk that talk boy, walk that walk boy
Spit that syrup in minds
Make em pay attention

Got me talking revolution
Knowing she loves the drama
Got me turning tricks
Into reality shows

My taxicab confession
Is that I don't want my passion
Stuck in this cowardly shell of a man
I want it to be driven in this black stretch limousine
Carrying the heart of a fucking star

I'm a whore to a lover some say
Doesn't give a damn about me
But I have faith in her

Because if you can't show me that roses
Can grow through concrete
Where everyone else has given up
Don't waste my time
"Trespassers will be prosecuted"
"No lifeguard on duty"
"No loitering"
"Private Property"
"Please use the other door"
I've lost my faith in signs
Drawn between my dual existence
As if the artist can be separated from the man
As if the African can be separated from the American
I've lost my faith in lines
Misery marches in unison
So tell me how to deal
With this pack of wild wolves
Crawling up my spine
I'm nervous

I want her to hold me
Tell me it's gone be all right
But no
She just wants me to keep her coming
Satisfy her narcissism
Make her the focus of my labor
Threatens me with overhand civil rights
And left crosses

Says
Get out there on them streets

Make that money
Lay down those words on those tracks
Freak them poems
They pay extra for the rough stuff
Make it feel real good
Touch souls
Massage them egos
Know when to be a jerk off
You worth more
Because of what you can do with that tongue
You pretty smart boy
You got a tight body of work
Show em what you got
Because you owe
You owe

Because of her
The world only knows me
When I am naked and willing
Vulnerable
But I'm sorry
Tell History I don't want to be
Her whore no more

Yet I find myself undressing
Preparing for this moment
I ain't desperate, I'm submissive
Dominated by my desire to matter
On this stage
Because you were willing to spend
A little time and a little money

Being introduced to what I can do with this pen
So I lay it all on the line
Let you have your way with my words
Hoping you ask for more
And when you leave
I'll wrap myself in my self-assurance
And pretend that I'm not a whore

Scream Black Man Scream

Scream black man scream
Like banshees howling at the night
Like black calm invading a white light
Make them bow to the power of determination
Make them quiver at the bellows
Of Tribal Kings and Queens
Bring those words from deep
Oral slaves trapped in the gallows
Of a divine vessel
Blessed with poise and filled with passion
Let your mouth be the middle passage
Words travel to work fields of thought
Scream black man scream

This was the poem written on a small parchment of cloth
His granddaddy gave him when he left
A young boy from the backwoods of Carolina
Now trudging the gutters of NY with one dream
He dreamed of the stage
He worked hard to get cast
But was too often type cast

Dark skinned like black berries
Drawl thick like molasses
Beautiful like songs sung under oak trees
But what they saw was ragged
Like an old tire swinging from a tree

Hung his dreams from that branch

Claimed he wasn't fit for shine
He wasn't supposed to touch that white light
Rejection after rejection

Hours spent going over his lines in his room
Small and cramped like his opportunity for a role
Other than the one stereotyped in bold font
Printed in black and white
Held that script in his hands
Felt his tomorrow was there in black and white

Optimism was on that parchment
The only thing his granddaddy learned to read
Raised on hard work
Worked hard on that farm to raise a family
Signed X's on important documents
Escaped burning crosses and hatred
To be a protector for his angel's first baby

See they don't give up where he's from
So he gone keep facing rejection
Until his big break comes
He only needed one
So he replaced hard times
With acts and scenes
Filled his head with lines
Etched them into his memory
Built a shield with steel will
So "no" could never be a weapon
Formed against him

Felt his dark skin helped him blend in
In the middle of the night
So he picked midnight to rehearse

Became good at playing characters
Moving man, busboy, stock clerk
He's been on stages
The black academic exception
The evidence of young black possibility
He's been mastering roles
Knew this was his destiny
The heavenly spirit directing his every step
God producing the devotion in his soul

Uses that parchment as inspiration
Remembers when it was tear stained
Mourning waterfalling when granddaddy passed
He was in NY chasing a falling star
Wishing he could have been there
Feeling he should be there
Because his granddaddy was the one who
Believed he could be here

Scream black man scream
Is what it said
So he hollered into the hollows of his spirit
Trapped angst there to fuel his desire
Prisoners rioting at ill gotten treatment
As "I'm sorry to inform you" letters
Lock down his promise like C.O.s
Banshees howling at the night

Like black calm invading a white light

That parchment was prophecy
As his words worked fields of thought
Until the day someone took notice
Helped him underground railroad his potential past
Undermining producers
Cast him as a lead
And opening night
He paid attention to one piece of advice
Remembered that piece of parchment
And when his name was called
After the final curtain call
He didn't bow to the standing ovation
He screamed

The Deck

Mother Nature whispers across my face
I smile at her fresh air flirtations
Look up at the sun looking back in jest
His cheshire grin beams
He knows we flirt like this often
I reach for my ipod
Headphones on
Thumb orchestrates this concert
Jazz compositions fill my head
I grab my glass of Moscato
Sip the sweetness slowly
Savor the satisfaction
Then return the glass to the table
The smell of cinnamon tickles my nose
But those rolls will have to wait
Words are marching out of my spirit
They are in procession to my right hand
Where they will meet at the page
Like white house lawn
Guided by this powerful black pen
I grab my notebook to receive them
Calmed by the beauty of this view from my deck
Blow a kiss to Mother Nature
Then begin
To write

Soda

10 blocks two times a day
To work 10 hours a day
Two ways to make ends meet
In this dirt or on the street
He chose a construction site laying bricks
So his family could build their tomorrows
On a strong foundation
Never had the tools to succeed in school
But he was good with the tools needed to build infrastructure
He didn't make it to that college institution
Until he was assigned to the project
To craft that institution's new building
His craft finally getting him to where
He always knew he should be
He was up before dawn
Both the sun that shined in the sky
And his baby girl whose smile was like sky
Kissed her sleeping face and whispered goodbye
I saw him every morning
Weight on his shoulders
Wanted him to know I understood
When he bought that Mountain Dew
That those misty eyes at the peak of breakdown knew pain
Frustration climbing to the summit of giving up
But responsibility ranged from his house to his mother's
Past due bills lining the skyline like clouds
He made this hike so his ends could meet
Left that worksite with exhaustion packed on his back
I saw him every evening
As the sun kissed the horizon
He ordered a Sunkist for the last block home
I knew he needed something to renew the bright in his spirit

I think of how happy he must feel
To walk through that door
See longing eyes welcoming home a hero
Kiss the sun that beams devotion into their relationship
Hold dawn in his arms now because tomorrow
He will be gone before she wakes
We have an unspoken understanding
I keep that 20 oz bottle cold
He keeps on walking
10 blocks two times a day
To work 10 hours a day
Two ways to make ends meet
In this dirt or on the street
And he couldn't choose the other
Left that behind long ago
When he stood outside this store
Orange Crush in his hands
Killing the light in addicted souls who couldn't resist the fix
On a good day he took back 2 or 3
Pulled in 2 or 3
Because baby was on the way, due date in 2 to 3
On a bad day it was an Orange Slice
Cut deep at the inadequate amount of money
He was taking home
Because when the horizon sliced into the sun
He had drunk the corner dry
But his pockets were thirsty for more
I hated seeing him this way
The streets drinking his potential away
Like he was soda

Daffodils

Summertime
Daffodils
Those were the words he repeated
Over and over again
Like a future prodigy
Practicing chord progressions
This melody was noted on charts
Read by nurses
Who couldn't read Mozart in his eyes
Just mo work in his care

Most of them grew annoyed
She grew curious
Young nurse age 26
Wondering what was behind
That Herculean smile
She knew took great effort
She didn't know
It had been stripped of its immortality long ago
Ended up in front of an Oracle of a physician
Who predicted that if he kept it up
It wouldn't be long before demise
Freed him from affliction

She sat at his bedside for 30 minutes each day
Holding his hand
Listening to Beethoven's Moonlight Sonata
She felt it matched the dark he was living in
This blue moon

Made ocean waves tidal along her cheeks
And only spoke two words
Summertime
Daffodils

She discovered he was a writer
His pseudonym was James Raine
Found his last interview online
When she stopped trying to fill in
The blank search field in his stare
And filled in the search field in Google
In it the reporter asked
About the progress of his latest book
He said it was all falling apart
Imagine the foreshadowing

It was the story of a
A young man
A young woman
Two writers
Who weaved words, held tongues, and tangled bodies
Found solace from the winter wind
Between sheets
He was looking for an escape
She was looking for a compass
Trying to find the right direction for her heart
He became an archetypal hero
She became his Summer Solstice
His longest day
Celebrated with a festival of kisses
His Shakespearean dream

That ended in tragedy when she decided
That theirs was an affair she couldn't carry on
When she left him
She told him she would always carry him in her soul
It took 10 years for him to find out
She carried to term a part of him in her womb
The letter said she looks just like you

James asked the reporter what do you do
When you have a child you can't picture meeting
Because the film of your relationship is underdeveloped
See I found solace in a bottle
Jim Bean, vicodin, xanax
To ease the pain of unreturned letters
Calm the anxiety of wondering
If I would ever know her laugh
Her smile

The nurse wondered
If James knew the story would end here
With him laying in that hospital bed
Like bad grammar
An incomplete sentence
Had a daughter he couldn't hold
So subject and verb didn't agree
The reporter asked James if he knew his daughter's name
He said her name was Daffney
Daffney Olivia Dillyson
Daffodils

When the nurse heard the code
She rushed back to his room
Ran to his beside
Held his hand tight
Looked him in his eyes
Told him don't give up
Summer can make flowers blossom
But rain makes flowers grow
Don't you dare leave this earth
Until you plant dew like kisses on her cheek
Seasons change
So why can't her mother
You can puddle yourself in this bed
Or imagine your daughter
Is somewhere dancing tribal dances
Trying to make the rain come
How can a writer
Not believe in edits
Don't you dare take the easy way out

When the orderlies pulled her out of the room
Ocean waves tidaling down her face
She shivered like Bach's cello strings
Chord progressions off her tongue
As she watched James write the last flat line
In his autobiography
She could only utter two words
Summertime
Daffodils

Marvin

How many great men
Are conceived while the devil's on vacation
Born when the devil takes a nap
See a blessing was given
To that ordained minister
An angel learned the notes of deliverance
In the house of God
Misunderstanding from his father's heavy hand
You drummed that rhythm of expression
Put finger to keys
Opened the door to our hearts

Play Marvin Play

Allow the holy trinity to guide you
That 3 octave voice that crooned sweet melodies
Never been uniform
Always unique
Didn't fit in that Air Force uniform
It left your purpose incomplete
Jets can't fly higher
Than the hopes of your fans
No Marvin you were supposed to play
Teach chocolate city the tone
Be the name on The Marquees
It's Okeh with me
Tell *Mama Loochie* it's all right
To shake her hips
Let the 10 commandments of love

Flow off your lips
See Marvin
You were a stubborn kind of fellow
Motown couldn't corral the greatness
God wanted you to sing
The devil wanted to play
Spent your lifetime trying to take your joy away
History still remembers the day
Your Precious Love collapsed in your arms
Ashford and Simpson couldn't write that away
Ain't nothing like the real thing
You're all I need to get by
Brings tears to your eyes
When Tammy ain't there
But you didn't lose your dreams
Sing Marvin sing
Play Marvin play
Even if the devil is taking Anna away
Mercy Mercy me
What's Going On
How did it all go so wrong?
You uplifted us during trying times
We couldn't see the hurt behind the songs
Then you found the answer
In a midnight refuge
Got *Sexual Healing*
Regained your hold
Gave the *Star Spangled Banner*
Some much needed soul
At the top of your game
Even though the cocaine was taking control

You just sang
Dammit boy you just sang
Laughed in Hell's face
See that bullet didn't take you away
You'll never be replaced
I heard you do a duet with Jay-Z
Just the other day
A smile came to my face
I said sing Marvin sing
Don't turn that off
Let that play
You taught us how to live, how to love
How to make love, how to make more
Now the devil can't rest
Spends his days in agony awake
Because he knows he made a mistake
Now I say we agonize him
To the end of days
Put that CD in
Listen to Marvin sing
Let it play
Let it play
Let it play

Carmen

Hebrews 12:1

That was his response
Eyes capturing the corner like a Gordon Parks photograph
Posed in the midst of his disdain
Was Carmen Jones
Not a model
An example in his eyes
Of innocence lost

Hebrews 12:1
"Therefore, since we are surrounded by such a great cloud
of witnesses, let us throw off everything that hinders and the
sin that so easily entangles, and let us run with perseverance
the race marked out for us."

I listened to his scripted commentary
Watching Carmen
No Dorothy Dandridge
But still a tragic mulatto
Waiting to be plucked from that corner
Like a card from the deck
Life had got good at playing hearts
Quick to cast this Queen of Spades out of its grasp
Put responsibility on someone else
She knew her role
Wait for action
Look into car windows for a Bellafonte or Phifer
Because they would put steel bracelets on her wrist

Take her from the only way she could make ends meet
The only steady relationship she had
Was with the police

Arrest record was a double album
Arms like a producer's hard drive
Full of tracks
Where was the reason, the logic
Sampling bedrooms
And looping empty orgasms
Back seat like Protools
Cats just wanted to beat but no substance
No wonder they were one hit wonders
Pimp like Jimmy Iovine
Making money off over accented masculinity
Shady dealings
Where the aftermath of her work was only 50 cent

Everyday Carmen made that pilgrimage
To that corner like Mt. Sinai
Looking to the heavens for redemption
Returning with ten $100 bills like commandments
The neighborhood watched it happen
Holding to their judgment like false idols
No faith in her salvation
I wanted something better for her
Wished for a trumpet sound
A voice loud as thunder
To instruct her escape
Hoped that the next car she jumped into
Would be driven by Donnie McClurkin

So that this saint who fell down
Could get updated on the possibilities
For her tomorrows

I didn't know why she lived this way
Grey dress and charcoal boots
Like she was draped in a storm cloud
Lost her sunshine years ago
When Daddy's little girl
Became the object of his devilish desires
Since she ran away
She's known blue uniforms but no blue skies

Carmen, I believe
That something more is waiting for you
This old man doesn't see a living example
A testimony waiting to be told
But I watch you like revival
Because your breakthrough will be biblical
I know how you survive
A back that familiar with bedsprings
Knows how to bounce back stiff
You walk straight, regal, and elegant

Carmen
They see a fallen angel
I see a miracle waiting to happen
They are afraid of your burning bush
But it's where men cry to God for release
These idle watchers could save you
Instead they would rather attack your character

Use bible verses as blinders
To ignore the light of promise in your eyes
I say they need to check that book again
That they've forgotten their own sins
I know
That upon this mountain
God gave this world
Through Carmen
A reminder of its own fallacy

Baby girl
You are worth more than the price of admission
This blockbuster should not be your claim to fame
Carmen
An Oscar is not your knight in shining armor
You should awarded an academy
Instead of jail cell or halfway house
Carmen
I wish that MGM stood for May God Move
I want to animate your prayers
Show you how that Dreamworks
These people only see a snapshot of your life
But I know those Pixar not the whole of you
They see the Devil in the director's chair
But ignore the role life has scripted for you
I know what they think of you
But these trials and tribulations won't last
Carmen
These critics can have their opinion
But you do not have to be typecast

The Sandbox

I have come to believe
That babysitting is a covert CIA plot
A sociological experiment to test new torture techniques
Because I promise anyone would talk
If they spent 30 min with Justin

A bright bubbly little hell-spawn
Part evil genius, part fanatic, part make-believe
A rebel without reason
Just for the hell of it

I am the one who gets to hang with him regularly
When my cousin needs a day off
I'm the responsible one and Justin likes me
No, Justin likes a willing adversary
I'm just savvy enough to hold his attention

He has friends
Wicked little people
Despicable little demons
Now don't get me wrong
They're all cute, endearing, and lovable
But about as innocent as 4 teenagers with red eyes
In a room that smells like Febreeze and Nag Champa

This is my burden
To bond with these wild wisps
So I decide to enjoy it
I put them in a controlled environment

Let them entertain me
And wonder if God laughs at my novel imitation

See I take them to the park
To them it's paradise
A place where they can roam free
And I can occupy them for free

They start at the merry go round
Each helping to push the wheel around
They negotiate their labor like trade unions

Justin is the pit boss
Rarely pushes while coordinating shifts
With promises of adequate return
I am his benefit package and he barters me easily
This little goblin's familial 401K
He plans to pilfer for his own gain like Citigroup

They switch to the Jungle Gym
These tyrants are like the UN Council
They feign solidarity and then turn on each other
Switching sides like mood rings

The slide is like an indulgent dip they all take
Over and over again
Smiling as they drop
Like hands into the coffers of the unnamed
It's symbolic of entitlement
The climb to the top
Is only so you can sit on your ass

And enjoy the ride

But the true pleasure, the greatest whim
Is to see them in the Sandbox
There are four of them
Settling into their respective corners of the box
Like settling into office

They begin to build nations
Each bringing their own special resources
They won't let any other kids settle there
And they negotiate their play

Justin is slick
His dolls…I mean action figures truly believe they matter
Kevin is the incessant dictator
Battered and broken toys reflect his denigrating ways
Chris is the manipulator
Stuck in barren sand with few things to call his own
He put snacks in his bag rather than toys
And barters his crude riches for access to other kids' things
It all looks so familiar

The other week Justin staged a coup
Like Roosevelt in Columbia, Wilson in Haiti,
Carter in Nicaragua
Obama and the Honduras
Chris called him a barf head
He put an embargo on Chris
Exchanged promises I'd take everyone to get ice cream
If they didn't take Chris' snacks

Leaving him with nothing to play with
I laughed

I believe babysitting is a covert plot by God
To show us the reality of our doing
A Central Intelligence that defines our Agency
In impressing our future
A glimpse into the possible repetition of sins
In an effort to make change
A wake up call

This park adventure plays like CNN
I report it to Justin's mother like Fox News
Slanting the story to make her feel better
Yet it stays in my spirit like investigative journalism
Searching my consciousness for the truth
I try to hide it like congressional cover ups
But I know what I've seen and heard
These four young rabid hobbits like surveillance evidence
Oliver Stone script my concern

See Justin is still bad as hell
My worry is that
In this world we have created
Correcting that
May make him less successful
But leaving him that way
May make him Secretary of State

TV Without You

A bottle of wine and an empty embrace
Had me sitting on the couch
Imitating her favorite activity
Remembrance had captured me
Replaying how she lit up at the sight
Now I search for a semblance of her fire
In the midst of these reality TV shows

I flip incessantly through the channels
Settling first on "For the Love of Barack"
Where beautiful ideals vie for love
And a man must choose the one for him
A well casted and Machiavellian scripted adventure

Barack was the manchurian candidate
Columbia U, Harvard Law
Community organizer, civil rights attorney
Eloquent speaker, avid writer
Party rocka, show stoppa, passion igniter

The ladies saw a nobel prize in his eyes
Overcome by the charm of his keynote address
Health Care, Economic Reform, Greenhouse Gas,
And Socialism
Each dressed in approval rating
Designed by public perception
Woven by the bias of US media
Put to work by right wing interest like sweat shop indigents

He gave them nicknames
A political rite of passage through congressional objection
Candy Striper, Catalyst, Sky, and Big Red
Each dressed for the occasion
In disparate hope of significance
Desire to be part of a melanin hued legacy

Click

Real housewives in DC was on
I couldn't understand Cindy McCain
Because she had tape on her face
NoH8 written on her cheek
A simile of her husband's grasp on reality
Distant from his views
I was confused because Bill Clinton
Had tape over his mouth too
Not in support of same sex marriage
Hillary liked it better that way
Seems he can't handle an actual black man
In the role he made so popular

Jill Biden was livid
Secretary of Education Arne Duncan
Was taking aim at the NBA and NCAA
Over graduating athletes
While we suck at graduating students
Our education system is falling apart
Inner city schools are being taped over
I'm sorry
Duct tape does not fix everything

Click

Political patsy
Well-used republican make up
Concealer for hiding campaign flaws
White out Sarah Palin
Gets an extreme makeover
They can't seem to hide her lack of dignity
She still believes them when they tell her
It's for the good of the conservative agenda
A Fox News spot and a weatherproof billboard
Won't give you back your soul

Click

Three women are sleep in Al Gore's bed
John Edwards tries to console him
As he paces the kitchen floor
Gore doesn't know how it made it this far
Information Technology, Environment Conservation, and
Drug Companies
Make strange bedfellows
Gore says he doesn't want advice from a Political Quagmire
He would rather talk to Quahog's Adam West
At least he could rely on a better character
Scott Brown walks by naked
Looks quite cosmopolitan
No one pays him any mind
They know he's a platform schizophrenic

Click

Candy Striper is ready for a change
Barack promises reform
She doesn't know
That there are two sets of congressional producers
Each wants this to go a different way
He tells Sky she's full of it and he knows it
For so long she has been gassed up
By corporate sugar daddies with deep pockets
Catalyst lays claim to his heart
Said she has been his focus
Stimulus is her attraction
No one can refuse her package
Big Red believes that their collective souls
Should be responsible for the production of their relationship
They say Barack leans toward Big Red
But she has little desire for someone who seeks
To be politically diffident
She calls Glen Beck on the phone
You lied…he is not Hugo Chavez

Click

Bill Clinton thinks that Walt Disney is part of a plot
To further the impact of Obama's presidency
With the release of "Prince and the Frog"
They put the tape back over his mouth

Click

Nigeria, Zimbabwe, and Kenya chase Gore down the street
They want him to claim responsibility
For fighting generic AIDS medicines for poor countries
Scott Brown shows up in his pickup truck
They ride past John Edwards
Running from his indiscretions
They do not stop
Gore gets a phone call from Sir Morris Strong
Scott Brown gets a call from Eharmony
They have new options for his daughters
He says he will see what kind of publicity he needs
After Leno

Click

Barack is making passes at Candy Striper
But can't seem to make any headway
His influence can't get anything moving
She feels he wants to strip away who she is
So she can be accepted
Sky is tired of being called a gold digger
She said she prefers Al Gore anyway
Big Red doesn't do centrists
She finds out his Mao tattoo was stick on
His beret was made in China
And the only Red Star he rocks with
Is the Heineken mixtape with Talib Kweli
And his special edition Chuck Taylors
Catalyst is where he puts his faith
Promising recovery and reinvestment
He thinks they can win at this relationship

She says she hasn't loved like this since Clinton

Click

I turn the TV off
Clarity slapping the hell out of nostalgia
I now remember why she is gone
I wanted answers
She had no clue
Yet stayed glued
To the foolishness
Of a scripted reality

See baby I know you're watching
Scanning the channels for an apparition of truth
I hope you find what you're looking for

I pour another glass of wine
Baby Girl
This one is for you

Vagabonds

They call homeless people vagabonds but I call them kin
Because my soul remembers
What it's like to wander aimlessly
In search of its origin, in search of its place
The house I was raised in was my only homeland
The only middle passage was the middle class existence
My mother hoped my passing grades would lead me to
But my soul never forgot

Slave barges and auction blocks
Black Codes and Venus Hottentots
Ask Eli Whitney if he knew he would divide a country
Like I ask the school system
If they know they divide a people
By fostering the production of ignorance to their history
But my soul never forgot

I'm a vagabond searching for its place, homeless
Rebelling against societal norms like Gabriel Prosser
Denmark Vesey, Nat Turner
But betrayed by my indifference
Dredd Scott, John Brown
I treat my journal like an abolitionist
Frederick Douglass my nightmares
Because my soul never forgot

I emerged myself in civil war and let my heart and mind fight
My insight found emancipation and my reconstruction began
Writing with a slave hand

Letting my heart send wisdom north
A great migration of understanding
Tell Plessey I still keep my ancestors separate but equal
To my existence here
Consciousness going through a renaissance like Harlem
Words flowing through my pen on that Black Star Line
Standing in the midst of a white page like the Scottsboro 9
See my soul never forgot

I Jackie Robinson ignorance, Alain Locke's New Negro
I Emmett Till fields of thought until a Greensboro 4 sits in
And a civil rights movement grows
This student of poetry
Nonviolently coordinates committees of foot and meter
Until you attempt to assassinate my characters
Like Malcolm or Martin
Then they riot on pages
Like Watts, Like LA
Cluster together black like panthers
I'll Stokely Carmichael these stanzas
Until they stand separate from the page
Then transform into Kwame Toure spoken word

I raise a fist in the air when thought runs dry
Return it to the page like a gavel
Thurgood Marshall my writer's block
Dammit I'm asking for a change
Tired of social experiments
When they give you free lunch, public school education,
And medicare
Yet will never tell you

That you have been infected with inadequate services
Y'all, Tuskegee is still happening
But my soul will never forget

You can't gentrify my intelligence with urban renewal
Pushing my street sense further away from my book sense
As if to insult my common sense
Dangling opportunity

I will not let you Cross Bronx Expressway
My consciousness
Imma Clive Campbell plug these poems into a mic stand
Then park and jam these words into your minds
Furiously fan these five fingers in the air
Drawing attention to the message
Hold your attention like they held L.A. hostage

No wonder the Dr. prescribed the chronic
Because Death Row seems to be the place their heroes go
Gil Scott says home is where the hatred is
I say I know it's true
But I'm going to take us back to where our pride is truth
Path our spirits back there
GPS our roots and set forth on the course
Navigate our way back to redemption

Follow me my kinfolk, my vagabonds
Cast aside your cardboard box
Tomb of capitalism and patriarchy
Corrugated trap of western sensibility
Our place is not on the curb of success

We will not accept where we have been cast
Considered lost and worthless
Begging for change
We will claim our deliverance
Rebel against all tribulation
We are powerful, amazing
I know our value
I know our worth
Because my soul never forgot

Chat

I heard her calling
Wrapped myself in the sheet from her bed
Danced like she did at family reunions
Out into the field behind the house
Sunlight glistened off her smile
In the midst of a calm blue
I call this Skype
A teary-eyed connection to her memory
Sent a request to chat
She wind whispered a hello
I raised her favorite bamboo walking stick
Grandma, I wanted you to know I'll be strong
Dug that stick into the ground
Wrapped the sheet around it at half mast
Honored the soldier of my fortune
With a 21 "I Love You" salute
Blew her the kisses
I used to put on her cheek
Made an appointment with an oak tree
To meet her here again next week

Remember Me

I remember going with my Nanny to Church. She dressed in white all Usher Board beautiful. I remember the AME church jumping with the choir in full swing. I was given peppermints to occupy me as everyone smiled at how cute I looked in my suit. I never paid much attention to much past the singing. I do remember some of the scripture readings. A lady in a big hat delivered them. I always thought…my nanny got bigger ones than that. I remember one…it was…

Psalms 34:17-19: Yes, the Lord hears the good man when he calls to Him for help, and saves him out of all his troubles. The Lord is close to those whose heart is breaking: He rescues those who are humbly sorry for their sins. The good man does not escape all troubles – he has them, too. But the Lord helps him in each and every one.

Now here I am back in this Church. No white dressed Angel to hold my hand. I've ushered my own transgressions and bored of ignorant indulgence. I remember the club was jumping last night. Choirs dressed in ill intention singing mischievous melodies. I got peppermints to keep my breath fresh and smiles at how cute I look in my outfit. I do remember some of the hurt I saw in the depths of women with big full eyes. I always thought…My nanny had bigger ones than that. I wonder if she can see me now. I know she brought me here today, brought me here to you.
Hello…

Remember me
I'm the brother in the 6th pew
You might not remember me too well

But I've got a problem
And I was told to come to you
See I've been struggling
And it's been going on for a while
It's been so hard to be optimistic
Almost impossible to smile
Life is weighing heavy
And my body's getting weak
My heart is racing
Thoughts are racing
I can no longer sleep
See I need help
Need a way through
I've been seeking a resolution
And someone recommended you
Remember me
I'm the brother in the 5th pew
Halfway to the front
Because I'm almost convinced
That it's the direction I should go
But every week I move one row up
And next week is worse than the last
Faith holds me steadfast
And I pray soon this too will pass
My job stresses me
My friends are in turmoil and disarray
Kept me out all last night and I almost missed today
That number on my dresser
Wants to corrupt my soul with lust
I walk in shame and smile in vain
I pass through my old neighborhood in disgust

My bills are long
By bank account is wrong
And the food in the fridge is gone
My conviction is faltering
I don't know how much longer I can stay strong
See I need help
Need a way through
And someone recommended you
Remember me
I'm the brother in the 3rd pew
Trying to get closer to you
Sleepwalking towards deliverance
Holding on to a fleeting dream
Where my days are beautiful
My nights are peaceful
Because with faith nothing is as hard as it seems
But reality wakes me from my peace
I'm holding on
Because I feel closer to the answer
When I come hear your word each week
I feel closer to salvation
See I've heard your name lots of times
Never really paid it full attention
And when I was in full swing
You never got mentioned
Now the devil got a good swing on me
Knocked my knees wobbly
My foundation is shaken
And I'm trying to stay steady
Leaning on you
Remember me

I'm the brother at the altar
Broken down and humble
In recognition that my way
Was the wrong way
That I could try to find refuge
In this world
But needed to find refuge in you
I can't make it any other way
See you knew the saint inside that I just couldn't see
The prophet with a pen you knew I'd be
Covered and anointed by the hands of the father
Shielded from inequity so no weapon formed can prosper
Taught to be humble and always be thankful
Showed me the way of the faithful
So I pray
And be ever so grateful
That you remembered me

Home Improvement

Revolution
is the determination to climb
through the rubble
when your foundation has crumbled.
Instead of wallow,
you build a home
for your redefined convictions
from the pieces.
Etch "rebel" into the mailbox.

Architecture
is of no concern.
The shape of things to come
isn't relevant.
Build with transparent Legos
so everyone can see
your will to survive.

Resist
wasting time with new Lowes.
Set your sights high.
Get your materials from your heart.
It's the place that knows your True Value.
The blue print is in your daydreams.
No need to seek refuge in anyone else,
you can do it yourself.

Efficiency
is important.

Don't waste your potential.
Keep the door closed on your doubts.
Close the windows to your insecurities.
Go green.
Recycle lessons from your elders.
Let love be organic.
Let the natural light of hope in you shine.
Conserve your energy,
you'll need it to reach your aspirations.

Plant willpower in your front yard,
it will grow into resolve.
Don't be afraid to cry happy tears.
Water works.
Why trim?
Hedge a large support system.
Turn fear and doubt on its side.
That's how you landscape.

Don't rent a false sense of security.
Don't mortgage your tomorrows
for immediate gratification.
A life on loan
is debt to a downfall.
Build your destiny
from the ground up.
Work with materials you can afford
until you build a you
you can't afford to live without.
Own your responsibility for your happiness
from the start.

This is not Sparta

I got lost in my imagination
Hypnotized by the swirl of my underwear in the dryer
Lost in a land or lore
Where my kingship is legend
My skill with a lead blade the subject of song
They say
My thoughts drip from that sword like blood
After a hero's thrust

I tap my weapon on the table
Searching for the next line
As the smell of detergent fills the air
I hear silver maidens
Quarters
Clapping for me as they fall from the change machine
A harem eager to do my bidding
I send some into Passion's chamber
Intensifying the heat encompassing my load
Then begin to fold my towels
Leaving my notebook in anticipation of my next move

My muse stands with me
Watching as I return to that page
Only to be greeted by inhibition
Delivering a message to me
I look this ignorant hurdle in the eye
As it tells me Writer's Block is coming
I have two options
Submit or fall

As my self-doubt tells me to practice patience
I turn to my muse
A nod reiterates my role
Lost socks watch from hidden crevices
As undergarments fold in fear
Static clings them to hope I can overcome
How dare you
Come into my moment
Insult my imagination
Doubt my creativity
And tell me my only option
Is fall slave to self-consciousness
This is SPARTA!

The time I have trained for
I am king here
I will not crumble or submit
I will make my stand
Leading metaphor, alliteration, imagery
To battle

Muse offers this wisdom
Poet
Come back with your poem
Or in it
Yes my muse
I only know one way to face tomorrow
Never be concerned with the day after my downfall

I circle around the Laundromat to think

Confused launderers ask where I'm going
On a friendly stroll
Me and my figurative elements
In the midst of my thought process
I meet contrived content
Sure that I would need its help
What good are you to me?

I question intention
You, what's your occupation
Cliché
You, what's your occupation
Regurgitated images
And you
Simplistic and uninspired meter
My God how could we succeed?
With tired stanzas, limp metaphors,
Unoriginal similes
Listen to the roar of warriors
My figurative elements
What do you do?
WE WRITE.... GOOD SH*T!
See my good short cut
I have more literary devices than you

As I fill my laundry bag my ideas race
Then I return to my notebook to make my stand
Writer's Block's minions come
We stand against them all
Self-consciousness issues a final ultimatum
You will not survive

We will blacken your optimism with arrows of trepidation
Then my insipid imbecile
We will write in the dark
Your effectiveness lies in the insecurity of the mind
Our determination lies in the dedication of the heart

The battle rages
Metaphor falls to the page
Imagery falls to the page
Before the last of my soldiers fall
I hurl my intolerance toward Writer's Block
Gash across its insignificance
As I pen a passionate ending
And message falls
Into the impact of my poem
This is destiny my muse
How I return my appreciation to you

I grab my laundry, my notebook, and exit
Letting the doors of the Laundromat close behind me
Leaving the launderers
To tell a tale of extraordinary penmanship
How I rose to the challenge
Sent Writer's Block into the pits of hell

To all of you I offer this moral
Don't ever lose your fight scribes
Know there are only two options
Come back to your purpose
With your poem
Or in it

Sleeping Beauty

She saw it all in a dream
Drifted off into labyrinth of learning
A historical maze of moments etched into her subconscious
Waters flowing through the Nile River
Kingdoms established in Nubia and Egypt
Wisdom written in distinct style
Art as beautiful as the morning sky
Philosophy and Astronomy
Feeding curious intellect

She felt pride in her mother
Land
Where cities of prominence grew along the Niger
Where empires reigned like Ghana and Ethiopia
Her mother has always birthed strength and courage

She heard songs
Sung in tongues so swift
To drums that played life rhythms
People existed to the beat
Thrived in the sound
As griots shared lessons
Held in their mouths
Like water in gourds

She heard cries
As the ocean ate fallen angels
Tribal futures
Captured by false promises

Enslaved in shackles and taken away
From the Cape of Good Hope

How ironic
Those precious jewels taken in chains
From momma's jewelry box
Then and now
Diamonds are still attached to pain

She doesn't want her dream to be a nightmare
Not when Ghana is so amazing
Not when Cape Town is so prominent
Not when Nairobi is so beautiful

She knows conflict
Sierra Leone, Rwanda, and Ethiopia
Ravaged by war
Nigeria and its battles with the barons of oil
The Democratic Republic of the Congo
Losing its grasp on its resources
South Africa's fight for freedom and liberation
Until a democratic election was finally held
Hope held in the hearts of many
Guns held in the hands of the ANC
Soweto will not be forgotten

She knows loss
As ghosts haunt her memory
Loved ones taken by AIDS
Grey clouds darkening the sky
Crying

She screams
Wakes
Face full of anguish and hurt

She turns
Looks out her window
Sees the clear night sky
Feels the cool calm breeze comfort her
Hears the sounds of her mother's voice

Her mother
Land
Still beautiful
Still rich in meaning
In resource
In resolve
She knows because she is at home in her arms

She will speak its majesty
Letting its legacy fall from her lips
Like water from gourds
Like wisdom from griots
Recalling history etched into her understanding
Destiny drawn on her insight
Portraits of promise hung on her spirit
She knows her mother's value
Knows the contours of her face
The ancestry in her features
She has seen it
In a dream

Miss Nature

Mommy, I don't mean to disrespect you
But you're lost
Intoxicated off fumes from corporate greed
Industrial pollution is the residue
Lining your veins
This greenhouse is where you orphaned me
The effect has me reeling

Pimped by the sun
You said he had your sol
Mistress to the moon
He rarely offered a full commitment
Just made tears tidal like waves
Gone before morning
Leaving behind an empty night's stand

I can't stand how sun works you
From dawn to dusk
Where everyone can see your shortcomings
It only lowers the price
Wish I could look him in the eye
But I can't stand the sight

He doesn't know you photosynthesis
His actions for evidence
Mommy, I see an opportunity for escape
I know you CO_2
Breathe for every dream demons try to take from you

They've developed cold hearts
And sad intentions
Blue printing your death certificate
Exotic is not the definition of the dance you do
When they make you strip malls to increase revenue
Making your tomorrows barren
When it used to be filled with blossoming dreams

Momma, I wanna call you Angel
They say that's a lie
Because heavenly bodies line the sky
Not the common ground on which we stand
I plow the dirt with fingertips
Because I've longed to hold your hand

I cry for them to stop assaulting you
Misogynists who litter your skin
Scarlet letter you "for lease" or "for sale"
Blacken your beauty with bruises like asphalt
Claim you mixed use for residence or retail

Bystanders call you a whore
So they don't have to accept responsibility for respecting you
Lust for certain seasons rather than appreciate the all of you
Flipping the pages of Urban Hiker and Great Outdoors
Like they don't know the meaning of objectification

I am ashamed
That some only want to get inside
Rather than know the insight you could provide
Lies filling your sky clouding your judgment

Covering their recognition whenever you cry

Others drive the countryside
Trying to discover the heart of you
Following fair weather friends
Down the same beaten path
Hit it and leave
Mommy, will you ever believe in love again

When I was a boy
Scouting my way to understanding
You were my imagination
My companion, my nurturer
But I cast you aside and now I'm sorry for the neglect
Pour out bottled water for the death of our innocence
Hoping to drown my regret

Dialectical Diatribe

I am not your auction block fetish
I am a poem
Off the tongue of a chapped lipped soothsayer
With buckteeth
Chomping at the bit to tell you
That ink spills just like oil
By the hand that put it there
Don't make your page an ocean
Mine a congressman's daughter's trust fund
Your perception of value is not a variant
When both pages are filled by the same crude inspiration
Don't paint my power and impact popular
It is purpose
It is a Roberta Flack vibrato and a Bob Dylan guitar riff
Both soulful and socially relevant
You will not martyr your malcontent
Scottsboro 9 my significance
Push people to believe someone else's words over mine
Then lock me into a category that I cannot escape

There is wisdom
In collard green concertos
Seasoned with fatback discernment
Cured in the southern sun
I feel out of place sometimes around you
Like a cherry orchard in the middle of a landfill
Ripe with the realization of how bad this world can be
When too many are near sighted with no long-term vision
Of what an artist should be

Quick to accept the attention
But slow to take on the responsibility
You can costume your compassion
But you can't dress up your insincerity
Or lack of understanding
Of what this world has shaped me to be
I am origami slave ship
Ancestry force folded into this imperialistic impotence
Where it makes sense to screw with people's lives
But not come to understand
The extent of the damage caused
Don't eroticize my craftsmanship
Can't you see?
We are all broken Macy's Christmas bowls
Fractured fragments of a forgone conclusion
Every good thing comes to an end
I want to pour you a bowl of cereal
Fill it with milk like Elmer's glue
Trying to restore the innocent adhesive you used to have
Make sure they're cheerios
So that as the cereal touches your lips
Those small puckers
Can kiss you comfortable in your own skin
So you don't battle your perception of what's under mine

For too long you have been
Living loud in silence
Never speaking to the heart of me
Dying to meet you
I want something more significant
But I believe you think

We're supposed to screw each other over
I don't want to contract a belief
That there is something against me
Hidden inside of you like Trojan horses
I don't want to be infected with malice
So I'm popping condom wrappers like oxicontin
Covering up my disgust
Swallowing my pride when the sun rises
Like morning after pills
So I don't conceive any conflict
Now I'm letting my pen fight
I have nicknamed it Emiliano Zapata
Because it's better to spit on your feet
Than live on your knees
I am here
A rooted sycamore
With poems like strange fruit hanging from my tongue
A label around my neck like an albatross
But I grow stronger and wiser
I am Lena Horne's raspy revolution
Josephine Baker's underappreciated brilliance
Lauryn Hill's misunderstood insanity
Dave Chappelle's radical refusal
Kanye West's self consciousness
Jay-Z's self confidence
Ginsberg's late night indulgences
Norman Rockwell's perfectly painted paradox
I am here
A poem
Just like you

I'm a punchline...words beaten into a page. I'm a hyperbole...a gross exaggeration of what blessings I deserve. I'm alliteration...repetitive mistakes with the first smile that follows an "I need you". I am personification...my mother's prayers given human characteristics. I am nothing but a literary device. So I write.

Write Free
Speak Free
Live Free

Made in the USA
Lexington, KY
05 November 2019

56542683R00050